ALSO BY JACK GILBERT

Refusing Heaven

The Great Fires

Monolithos

Views of Jeopardy

THE DANCE MOST OF ALL

THE DANCE MOST OF ALL

POEMS

JACK GILBERT

ALFRED A. KNOPF   NEW YORK   2009

THIS IS A BORZOI BOOK
PUBLISHED BY ALFRED A. KNOPF

Copyright © 2009 by Jack Gilbert

www.aaknopf.com

Knopf, Borzoi Books, and the colophon are registered
trademarks of Random House, Inc.

Library of Congress Cataloging-in-Publication Data
Gilbert, Jack, [date]
The dance most of all : poems / by Jack Gilbert.—1st ed.
p.   cm.
ISBN 978-0-307-27076-4
I. Title.
PS3557.I34217D36 2009
811'.54—dc22   2008044670

Manufactured in the United States of America
First Edition

For Linda Gregg

CONTENTS

EVERYWHERE AND FOREVER   3

PAINTING ON PLATO'S WALL   4

ALYOSHA   5

WINTER IN THE NIGHT FIELDS   6

OVID IN TEARS   7

THE SPELL CAST OVER   8

SOUTH   10

NEGLECTING THE KIDS   11

DREAMING AT THE BALLET   12

ELEGY   13

AFTER LOVE   14

WAITING AND FINDING   15

WINTER HAPPINESS IN GREECE   16

MEANWHILE   17

THE ABUNDANT LITTLE   18

WORTH   19

PERFECTED   20

LIVING HUNGRY AFTER   21

THE MISTAKE   22

A FACT   23

BECOMING REGARDLESS   24

THE SECRET   26

THE NEW BRIDE ALMOST VISIBLE IN LATIN   27

THE DANGER OF WISDOM   28

SEARCHING FOR IT
IN A GUADALAJARA DANCE HALL   29

TRIANGULATING   30

THE DIFFICULT BEAUTY   31

GROWING UP IN PITTSBURGH   32

INFECTIOUS   33

PIECING OF THE LIFE   34

NOT EASILY   35

CROSSING THE BORDER,
SEARCHING FOR THE CITY   36

CRUSOE ON THE MOUNTAIN
GATHERING FAGGOTS   38

SUMMER AT BLUE CREEK, NORTH CAROLINA   39

GOING HOME   40

GETTING IT RIGHT   41

ALONENESS   42

FEELING HISTORY   44

TO KNOW THE INVISIBLE   45

PROSPERO GOES HOME   46

NAKED WITHOUT INTENT   47

TRYING   48

THE ANSWER   49

THE GROS VENTRE   50

WAKING AT NIGHT   52

CHERISHING WHAT ISN'T   53

VALLEY OF THE SPIRITS   54

SUDDENLY ADULT   55

WE ARE THE JUNCTION   56

THE DANCE MOST OF ALL

It pleases him that the villa is on a mountain
flayed bare by the great sun. All around
are a thousand stone walls in ruin. He likes knowing
the house was built by the king's telegrapher.
"To write at a distance." He keeps the gate closed
with a massive hasp and chain. The weeds inside
are breast-high around the overgrown rosebushes
and two plum trees. Beyond that, broad stairs
rise to a handsome terrace and the fine house
with its tall windows. He has excavated most
of the courtyard in back. It's there they
spent their perfect days under a diseased
grape arbor and the flowering jasmine. There is
a faint sound of water from the pool over by
the pomegranate tree with its exaggerated fruit.
The basin is no longer choked by the leaves
accumulated in the twelve years of vacancy.
He has come to the right place at the right time.
The blue Aegean is far down, and the slow ships
far out. Doves fly without meaning overhead.
He and the Japanese lady go out the back gate
and up the stream stone by stone, bushes on each side
heavy with moths. They come out under big plane trees.
There is a dirt path from there to a nunnery.
She says goodbye and he starts down to the village
at the bottom where he will get their food for a week.
The sky is vast overhead. Neither of them knows
she is dying. He thinks of their eleven years together.
Realizes they used up all that particular time
everywhere in the cosmos, and forever.

The shadows behind people walking
in the bright piazza are not merely
gaps in the sunlight. Just as goodness
is not the absence of badness.
Goodness is a triumph. And so it is
with love. Love is not the part
we are born with that flowers
a little and then wanes as we
grow up. We cobble love together
from this and those of our machinery
until there is suddenly an apparition
that never existed before. There it is,
unaccountable. The woman and our
desire are somehow turned into
brandy by Athena's tiny owl filling
the darkness around an old villa
on the mountain with its plaintive
mewing. As a man might be
turned into someone else while
living kind of happy up there
with the lady's gentle dying.

ALYOSHA

The sound of women hidden
among the lemon trees. A sweetness
that can live with the mind, a family
that does not wear away. He will let
twenty lives pass and choose the twenty-
first. He longs to live married to
slowness. He lives now with the lambs
the minute they are being born,
lives with their perfection as they
blunder around right away in pure innocence.
He watches them go up the mountain
each morning with the twelve-year-old
nearly child. Living with his faith
as he watches them eaten at Easter
to celebrate Christ. He is not innocent.
He knows the shepherdess will be given
to the awful man who lives at the farm
closest to him. He blesses all of it
as he mourns and the white doves soar
silently in the perfect blue sky.

I was getting water tonight
off guard when I saw the moon
in my bucket and was tempted
by those Chinese poets
and their immaculate pain.

OVID IN TEARS

Love is like a garden in the heart, he said.
They asked him what he meant by garden.
He explained about gardens. "In the cities,"
he said, "there are places walled off where color
and decorum are magnified into a civilization.
Like a beautiful woman," he said. How like
a woman, they asked. He remembered their wives
and said garden was just a figure of speech,
then called for drinks all around. Two rounds later
he was crying. Talking about how Charlemagne
couldn't read but still made a world. About Hagia
Sophia and putting a round dome on a square
base after nine hundred years of failure.
The hand holding him slipped and he fell.
"White stone in the white sunlight," he said
as they picked him up. "Not the great fires
built on the edge of the world." His voice grew
fainter as they carried him away. "Both the melody
and the symphony. The imperfect dancing
in the beautiful dance. The dance most of all."

In the old days we could see nakedness only
in the burlesque houses. In the lavish
theaters left over from vaudeville,
ruined in the Great Depression. What had been
grand gestures of huge chandeliers
and mythic heroes courting the goddess
on the ceiling. Now the chandeliers were grimy
and the ceilings hanging in tatters. It was
like the Russian aristocrats fleeing
the Revolution. Ending up as taxi drivers
in Paris dressed in their worn-out elegance.
It was like that in the Pittsburgh of my days.
Old men of shabby clothes in the empty
seats at the Roxy Theater dreaming
of the sumptuous headliners
slowly discarding layers of their
lavish gowns. Baring the secret
beauty to the men of their season.
The old men came from their one room
(with its single, forbidden gas range)
to watch the strippers. To remember what used
to be. Like the gray-haired men of Ilium
who waited each morning for Helen
to cross over to the temple in her light raiment.
The waning men longed to escape from the spell

cast over them by time. To escape the imprisoned
longing. To insist on dispensation. To see
their young hearts just one more time.
Those famous women like honeycombs. Women moving
to the old music again. That former grace of flesh.
The sheen of them in the sunlight, to watch
them walking by the sea.

SOUTH

In the small towns along the river
nothing happens day after long day.
Summer weeks stalled forever,
and long marriages always the same.
Lives with only emergencies, births,
and fishing for excitement. Then a ship
comes out of the mist. Or comes around
the bend carefully one morning
in the rain, past the pines and shrubs.
Arrives on a hot fragrant night,
grandly, all lit up. Gone two days
later, leaving fury in its wake.

For Susan Crosby Lawrence Anderson

He wonders why he can't remember the blossoming.
He can taste the brightness of the sour-cherry trees,
but not the clamoring whiteness. He was seven in
the first grade. He remembers two years later when
they were alone in those rich days. He and his sister
in what they called kindergarten.
They played every day on the towering
slate roofs. Barefoot. No one to see them on
those fine days. He remembers the fear
when they shot through the copper-sheeted
tunnels through the house. The fear
and joy and not getting hurt. Being tangled
high up in the mansion's Bing cherry tree with
its luscious fruit. Remembers
the lavish blooming. Remembers the caves they
built in the cellar, in the masses of clothing and draperies.
Tunnels to each other's kingdom with their stolen
jewelry and scarves. It was always summer, except for
the night when his father suddenly appeared. Bursting
in with crates of oranges or eggs, laughing in a way
that thrilled them. The snowy night behind him.
Who never brought two pounds of anything. The boy remembers
the drunkenness but not how he felt about it,
except for the Christmas when his father tried to embrace
the tree when he came home. Thousands of lights,
endless tinsel and ornaments. He does
not remember any of it except the crash as his father
went down. The end of something.

The truth is, goddesses are lousy in bed.
They will do anything it's true.
And the skin is beautifully cared for.
But they have no sense of it. They are
all manner and amazing technique.
I lie with them thinking of your
foolish excess, of you panting
and sweating, and your eyes after.

ELEGY

The bird on the other side of the valley
sings *cuckoo cuckoo* and he sings back, inside,
knowing what it meant to the Elizabethans.
Hoping she is unfaithful now. Delicate
and beautiful, making love with the Devil
in his muggy bedroom behind the shabby office.
While he is explaining the slums were there
when he got the job. *And* the Buicks burning
by the roads in the dark. He was not the one
doing the judging, he says. Or the one pointing down
at the lakes of burning lead. He is feeding
her lemons. Holding shaved ice in his mouth
and sucking her nipples to help with the heat.

AFTER LOVE

He is watching the music with his eyes closed.
Hearing the piano like a man moving
through the woods thinking by feeling.
The orchestra up in the trees, the heart below,
step by step. The music hurrying sometimes,
but always returning to quiet, like the man
remembering and hoping. It is a thing in us,
mostly unnoticed. There is somehow a pleasure
in the loss. In the yearning. The pain
going this way and that. Never again.
Never bodied again. Again the never.
Slowly. No undergrowth. Almost leaving.
A humming beauty in the silence.
The having been. Having had. And the man
knowing all of him will come to the end.

While he was in kindergarten, everybody wanted to play
the tom-toms when it came time for that. You had to
run in order to get there first, and he would not.
So he always had a triangle. He does not remember
how they played the tom-toms, but he sees clearly
their Chinese look. Red with dragons front and back
and gold studs around that held the drumhead tight.
If you had a triangle, you didn't really make music.
You mostly waited while the tambourines and tom-toms
went on a long time. Until there was a signal for all
triangle people to hit them the right way. Usually once.
Then it was tom-toms and waiting some more. But what
he remembers is the sound of the triangle. A perfect,
shimmering sound that has lasted all his long life.
Fading out and coming again after a while. Getting lost
and the waiting for it to come again. *Waiting* meaning
without things. Meaning love sometimes dying out,
sometimes being taken away. Meaning that often he lives
silent in the middle of the world's music. Waiting
for the best to come again. Beginning to hear the silence
as he waits. Beginning to like the silence maybe too much.

The world is beyond us even as we own it.
It is a hugeness in which we climb toward.
A place only the wind knows, the kingdom
of the moon which breathes a thousand years
at a time. Our soul and the body hold each other
tenderly in their arms like Charles Lamb
and his sister walking again to the madhouse.
Hand in hand, tears on their faces, him carrying
her suitcase. Blow after blow on our heart
as we grope through the flux for footholds,
grabbing for things that won't pull loose.
They fail us time after time and we slide back
without understanding where we are going.
Remembering how the periodic table of the elements
didn't fit the evidence for half a century.
Until they understood what isotopes were.

MEANWHILE

It waits. While I am walking through the pine trees
along the river, it is waiting. It has waited a long time.
In southern France, in Belgium, and even Alabama.
Now it waits in New England while I say grace over
almost everything: for a possum dead on someone's lawn,
the single light on a levee while Northampton sleeps,
and because the lanes between houses in Greek hamlets
are exactly the width of a donkey loaded on each side
with barley. Loneliness is the mother's milk of America.
The heart is a foreign country whose language none
of us is good at. Winter lingers on in the woods,
but already it looks discarded as the birds return
and sing carelessly; as though there never was the power
or size of December. For nine years in me it has waited.
My life is pleasant, as usual. My body is a blessing
and my spirit clear. But the waiting does not let up.

We have seen the population of Heaven
in frescoes. Dominions and unsmiling saints
crowded together as though the rooms were small.
We think of the grand forests of Pennsylvania,
oaks and maples, when we see the miniatures
of blue Krishna with farm girls awkwardly
beside a pond in a glade of scrub trees.
The Japanese scrolls show mostly Hell.
When we read about the Christian paradise,
it is made of gold and pearls, built on
a foundation of emeralds. Nothing soft
and rarely trees, except in the canvases
of Italians where they slip in bits of Tuscany
and Perugino's Umbria. All things
are taken away. Indeed, indeed.
But we secretly think of our bodies
in the heart's storm and just after.
And the sound of careless happiness.
We touch finally only a little.
Like the shy tongue that comes fleetingly
in the dark. The acute little that is there.

WORTH

It astonished him when he got to Katmandu to hear
the man from the embassy say a friend was waiting
outside of customs. It was the Australian woman
he had met in Bali. His fault for running back
across the tarmac when he realized she was crying.
Kissing her while the plane waited with the door open.
Wanting her to feel valuable. Now she had used up all
her money flying to Nepal. In trouble because
we can't parse the heart. Calling what had been
what it was not. Now lying awkwardly on the bed
for a month, marooned in the heat, the Himalayas
above the window. As he watched the delicate dawns
and the old women carrying too much firewood down
from the mountain on their backs. Him thinking of their
happiness up in the lush green terraces of rice.
Remembering her laughter as he came out of the shower,
saying the boy had come again with a plate of melon.
"He asked if you were my husband," she said, "and I
said you were my father." Her eyes merry. Now they sat
in cheap restaurants trying to find anything to say.
Remembering how beautiful she was the first time
coming through the palm trees of the compound at dusk.
Tall and thin in a purple dress that reached to her
bare feet. Watching while he played chess with
the Austrian photographer all night. Now calling
that good thing by the wrong name. Destroying
something valuable. Innocently killing backwards.

PERFECTED

In the outskirts of the town
the street sweeper puts down
his broom of faggots and angrily
begins to shake the young ginkgo.
The leaves fall faster.
He shakes it even harder
and the leaves fall by ones and twos.
He rests to calm himself.
A passing boy speeds up
and leaps in the air,
slamming the trunk with both feet.
The yellow leaves spurt out.
The three of them stand looking up.
One leaf falls, then more.

The water nymphs who came to Poseidon
explained how little they desired to couple
with the gods. Except to find out
whether it was different, whether there was
a fresh world, another dimension in their loins.
In the old Pittsburgh we dreamed of a city
where women read Proust in the original French,
and wondered whether we would cross over
into a different joy if we paid a call girl
a thousand dollars for a night. Or an hour.
Would it be different in kind or only
tricks and apparatus? I worried that a great
love might make everything else an exile.
It turned out that being together
at twilight in the olive groves of Umbria
did, indeed, measure everything after that.

There is always the harrowing by mortality,
the strafing by age, he thinks. Always defeats.
Sorrows come like epidemics. But we are alive
in the difficult way adults want to be alive.
It is worth having the heart broken,
a blessing to hurt for eighteen years
because a woman is dead. He thinks of long
before that, the summer he was with Gianna
and her sister in Apulia. Having outwitted
the General, their father, and driven south
to the estate of the Contessa. Like an opera.
The fiefdom stretching away to the horizon.
Houses of the peasants burrowed into the walls
of the compound. A butler with white gloves
serving chicken in aspic. The pretty maid
in her uniform bringing his breakfast each
morning on a silver tray: toast both light
and dark, hot chocolate and tea both. A world
like *Tosca*. A feudal world crushed under
the weight of passion without feeling.
Gianna's virgin body helplessly in love.
The young man wild with romance and appetite.
Wondering whether he would ruin her by mistake.

A FACT

The woman is not just a pleasure,
nor even a problem. She is a meniscus
that allows the absolute to have a shape,
that lets him skate however briefly
on the mystery, her presence luminous
on the ordinary and the grand. Like the odor
at night in Pittsburgh's empty streets
after summer rain on maples and sycamore.
As well as the car suddenly crossing two blocks
away in a blare of light. The importance
of the rocks around his Greek shepherd hut,
and mules wandering around in the empty fields.
He crosses the island in the giant sunlight,
comes back in the dark thinking of the woman.
The fact of her goes on, loved or not.

I begin to see them again as the twilight darkens.
Gathered below me and to the right under the tree.
Ghosts are by their nature drawn to the willows.
They have no feet and hover just above the grass.
They seem to be singing. About apples, I think,
as I remember the ones a children's red in the old
cemetery in Syracuse where I would eat one each day
because the tree grew out of a grave and I liked
to think of someone eating what was left of my heart
and spirit as I lay in the dark earth translating
into fruit. I can't be sure what they are singing
because no sound comes through the immense windows
of my apartment. (Except for the sound somebody
makes at two and four in the night as he passes
around what was the temple grounds hitting a block
of wood two or three times with a stick. I have
begun listening for it as I lie on the floor awake.)
I try to see in what is left of the light down there
the two I was. The ghost of the boy in high school
just before I became myself. The other is the ghost
of the times later when I could fall in love:
the first time, and three years after that for eight
years, and the last time ten years after. I feel
a great tenderness for all the dozen ghosts down
there trying to remain what they were. Behind each
pile of three boulders that are the gravestones
is a railing making an enclosure for the seven-foot,
narrow, unpainted planks with prayers written on them.
They are brought on the two ceremonial days each year
by the mourners and put with the earlier ones. But

in many enclosures there are just weathered old ones,
because they are brought only as long as there is
still someone who knew the dead. It puzzles me that
I care so much for the ghost of the boy in high school,
since I am not interested in those times. But I know
why the other one frightens me. He is the question
about whether the loves were phantoms of what existed
as appearance only. I know how easily they come,
summoned by our yearning. I realize the luminosity
can be a product of our heart's furnace. It would
erase my life to find I made it up. Then I see them
faintly dancing in the dark: spirits that are the invisible
presence of what those women were. There once was
a Venezia even if there is not now. The flesh thickens
or wanes, but there was somebody I knew truly. Three
of them singing under the willow inside my transience.

THE SECRET

There is an easy beauty in the bronze statues
dredged up from the ocean, but there is a worth
to the unshapely our sweet mind founders on.
Truth is like a pearl, Francis Bacon said.
It is lovely in clear light, but the carbuncle
is more precious because its deep red shows best
in varied illumination. "A mixture of a lie
doth ever add pleasure." When the Chinese made
a circle of stones on the top of their wells,
one would be a little skewed to make the circle
look more round. Irregularity is the secret
of music and to the voice of great poetry.
When a man remembers the beauty of his lost love,
it is the imperfect bit of her he remembers most.
The blown-up Parthenon is augmented by its damage.

We want to believe that what happens
in the dark bedroom is normal.
Pretending that being alive
is reasonable keeps the door shut
against whether maggots, nematodes,
and rot are also created in God's image.
Our excess is measured, our passion
almost deliberate. As we grow up,
we more and more love appropriately.
When Alicia got married, the priest
conducted the Mass in English because
it was understandable. He faced us
as though we were friends. Had us
gather around the altar afterwards.
She hugged and kissed each one until me.
The bride, fresh from Communion,
kissed me deeply with her tongue,
her husband three feet away.
The great portals of our knowing
each other closed forever. I was flooded
by the size of what had ended.
But it was the mystery of marriage
and its hugeness that shocked me,
fell on me like an ox. I felt
mortality mixing with the fragrance
of my intimacy with her. The difference
between the garden of her body
and the presence of her being was the same
distance as the clear English of the Mass from
the blank Latin which held the immensities.

We learn to live without passion.
To be reasonable. We go hungry
amid the giant granaries
this world is. We store up plenty
for when we are old and mild.
It is our strength that deprives us.
Like Keats listening to the doctor
who said the best thing for
tuberculosis was to eat only one
slice of bread and a fragment
of fish each day. Keats starved
himself to death because he yearned
so desperately to feast on Fanny Brawne.
Emerson and his wife decided to make
love sparingly in order to accumulate
his passion. We are taught to be
moderate. To live intelligently.

SEARCHING FOR IT
IN A GUADALAJARA DANCE HALL

You go in from the cobbled back street.
Into an empty, concrete one-room building
where prim youngish women sit in a line
of straight chairs. The women are wearing
tea dresses thrown away by rich Texan
women two generations ago. The men are
peasants, awkward in a line of chairs opposite.
Nothing is sexual. There are proprieties.
No rubbing against anyone. No touching
at all. When the music starts, the men
go stiffly over to the women. It isn't
clear whether they say anything. The dance is
a slow, solemn fox trot. When it stops,
they stand still while the men
find a coin. The women stow it and all
of them go back to the chairs to wait for
the music and another partner. This is
not for love. The men can get love
for two coins at a shack in the next field.
They know about that. And that they will
never be married, because it is impossible
to own even a little land. They are
groping for something else, but don't know what.

TRIANGULATING

All taken down like Trastevere or København.
Like her apartment on Waller in San Francisco
or their place on Oak. The ruined cities
of America. The grand theaters built for vaudeville,
tawdry and soiled when he knew
them in Baltimore and Chicago. Full of
raggedness and a band. Calumet City when
it was a mob town with public vice.
A scale visible in the decay. Something
to measure against. Night after night
walking the Paris he knew. Hôtel Duc de Bourgogne
on Île Saint-Louis, the room
with a stone floor on the rue Boutarel across from
the cathedral. The old building where
his mansard was on a hill above the canal.
All taken down. Places that were clues
for a moment when he understood.
Knew the name of our quarry.
The something we were changing into.

The air full of pictures no matter where you reach in.
Vast caverns in the ground bright with electricity
and covered everywhere with language. Because you
live on the fourth floor, you can on Sundays look
down into the synagogue across the street where people
sing secretly together in Spanish. You are up there
trying to get the galleys marked which are so late
(because of love) that Yale threatens not to publish
the book at all. Noise so loud you finally look
outside and see everybody gathered on Fourth Street
near Avenue C to eat ice cream and watch the guys
carrying a naked woman down the fire escape clumsily
who had been promising all morning to jump. But best
of all are the gardens: hidden places where they have
burned down the buildings and kept the soil
poor so the plants won't grow with vulgar abundance.
Like the Japanese gardens made only of rocks and sand
so their beauty would not be obscured by appearances.
Like the maharaja who set aside the best courtyards
in his palace for the dandelions he imported from
England to be kept alive by the finest gardeners
in the world who knew how to work against nature.

Go down to the drugstore at the corner,
it said. At the drugstore it said,
Go to the old woman's house. On her porch
was scribbled: Where has love gone?
To the arcades of the moon, I wrote.
To the Palladian moon, and is embezzled
there as well. Therefore are the gunwales
of my heart plated. For the birds
have rings on their necks and must
take the catch to the white boats
at the marble pier in exchange for gruel.
Old hoplites cursing under the arcades
snap the pale fish and wrap them in plundered
drawings. A whimpering leaks from the bundles,
from the stalls, into the piazza and up
to the roof where everyone in the shining
is watching a performance of romance.

INFECTIOUS

I live with the sound my body is,
with the earth which is my daughter.
And the clean separation which is my wife.
There is no one who can control us
because we live secretly under the ocean
of each day. Except for the music.
The memory of rainy afternoons
in San Francisco when I would play
all the slow sections of Mozart's
piano concertos. And the sound
of the old Italian peasant who occasionally
came down from the mountain to play
a primitive kind of guttural bagpipe,
and sometimes sing with his broken voice
in the narrow lanes about the moon
and the grief of lovers. That reedy sound
is stuck in me. Like the Japanese monk
who would come through the graveyard
at night striking two sticks together.
I can't forget the pure sound I heard once
when a violin string snapped nearby
in three o'clock's perfect silence.
But I tell myself I'm safe. I remind myself
of the boy who discovered order in the piano
and ran upstairs to tell his little sister
that they didn't have to be afraid anymore.

The man wondered if he had become
like Di Stefano, when he was no longer able
to sing the best of Verdi. He knew how better
than anyone, but finally didn't have the strength
for Othello. My friend's wife had left him
and he wondered if he could still hold the world
in his arms. And would he know if his quiet
was the beginning of decline. He talked often
of the first girl he kissed, when he was sixteen.
He had not been prepared for the velvety
plushness. We watched the evening begin.
"Fifty and waning," he said. Touched my arm and we
walked slowly back. Silent and wonderfully content.

NOT EASILY

When we get beyond beauty and pleasure,
to the other side of the heart (but short
of the spirit), we are confused about what
to do next. It is too easy to say arriving
is enough. To pretend the music
of the mountain needs only to be heard.
That the dance is known by the dancing,
and the lasagne is realized by eating it.
Not in this place on the other side
of desire. We can swim in the Aegean,
but we can't take it home. A man finds
a melon by the road and continues up
the hill thinking it is the warm melon
that will remain after he has forgotten
the ruins and sea of the summer. He tells
himself this even as the idea of the taste
is replacing what the melon tasted like.

CROSSING THE BORDER,
SEARCHING FOR THE CITY

He thought of the boy in the middle
of the poison gas. The gas mask dangerously
slipping on his face, because he was sweating
so much. ("Death on all sides.") Fear all through him,
but also the excitement from his intruding,
because of the privacy he had penetrated.
The hidden world he was not part of.
Glimpsed all his life in the windows he walked past
at night. The young mother dancing slowly
with her little daughter. The teenager preening
in her new dress in front of her father.
The world without him he was seeing as he
opened cupboards and pulled clothes
from the bureaus. Drawers of the daughter's
mysterious underclothes. What they had on
the dresser. Curiously the same as his rummaging
earlier in the refrigerator for the food
to put on the porch. Finding what had gotten
lost, shriveled, or spoiled. All his life wondering
what reality was, without his presence.
Lying in somebody's side lawn, the night rain
coming down and the smell of lilacs
as he watched a family eating dinner in their light.
Later the Hispanic women in the Laundromats.
And in Rome, when he lived with the peasants
from Calabria. Never a part of it

despite their friendship. Now in the village
of black magic with tokens among the trees
announcing which paths led to death. Trying
to decide about the Australian woman
beside him. The borders again, he thinks,
remembering the woman in København he had
never seen as he slid out of the terrible
cold into her sleepy warmth. Her face
invisible in the dark. The soft sound
she made welcoming him wordlessly,
utterly. Into the great light of her body.

CRUSOE ON THE MOUNTAIN
GATHERING FAGGOTS

He gets dead sage and stalks of weeds mostly.
Oleander can kill a fire, they say.
The length of valley below is green
where the grapes are. The small farms
of wheat tiny. And two separate cows.
Then the sea. Here's a terraced mountain
abandoned to bracken and furze and not
even that. If there was water once,
there isn't now. Rock and hammering sun.
He tastes all of it again and again,
his madeleine. He followed that clue
so long it grew faint. Which must account
for his happiness in this wrong terrain.

There was no water at my grandfather's
when I was a kid and would go for it
with two zinc buckets. Down the path,
past the cow by the foundation where
the fine people's house was before
they arranged to have it burned down.
To the neighbor's cool well. Would
come back with pails too heavy,
so my mouth pulled out of shape.
I see myself, but from the outside.
I keep trying to feel who I was,
and cannot. Hear clearly the sound
the bucket made hitting the sides
of the stone well going down,
but never the sound of me.

GOING HOME

Mother was the daughter of sharecroppers.
And my father the black sheep of rich Virginia
merchants. She went barefoot until twelve.
He ran away with the circus at fourteen.
Neither one got through grammar school.
And here I am in the faculty toilet
trying to remember the dates of Emperor Vespasian.

GETTING IT RIGHT

Lying in front of the house all
afternoon, trying to write a poem.
Falling asleep.
Waking up under the stars.

Deep inside the night on the eighth floor.
Scared to be alone with him in his room.
Hoping the drug still controls his violence.
The massiveness of him. The girth
of the wrist as he holds it. And the sound
of his heart. In the corridor outside,
blank eyes at each of the small windows.
The silence getting denser and denser
as it continues farther away.

Everywhere the sighing of the beds
rocking slowly, steadily, eternally
in the hushed dimness as he reaches in
to the hot bed of the contagious fat woman
to turn her over. Him frightened in
the paper clothes and a mask.

They give him a dead woman swathed
tightly in loop after loop of brown tape,
from the crown of her head down
to the toes. Like a mummy under water.
Wrestling with it in the concrete basement.
The weight of her slack body pulling
out of his arms. Lifting her with difficulty
by hugging the body against him. Shocked
at the dead thing's heat. Fighting to get
her into the immaculate drawer. The sound
of steel sliding on steel.

The straight-edge razors they use on Saturday nights slash so fast and clean there is no pain. They fight on without noticing the mutilation. Ears gone, noses carved, cheeks laid bare. Standing in line later to be neatly staunched and stitched.

Got up before the light this morning
and went through the sweet damp chill
down to the mindlessly persisting sea.
Stood neck-deep in its strength thinking
it was the same water young Aristotle
knew before he stopped laughing.
The cold waves came in on me,
came in as the sun went from red
to white. All the sea turned blue
as I walked back past the isolate
shuttered villa.

The Americans tried and tried to see
the invisible Indians in the deeper jungle
of Brazil. Finally they put things in the clearing
and waited. They waited for months,
maybe for years. Until a knife and a pot
disappeared. They put out other things
and some of those vanished. Then one morning
there was a jungle offering sitting on the ground.
Gradually they began to know the invisible
by the jungle's choices. Even when nothing
replaced the gifts, it was a kind of seeing.
Like the woman you camp outside of, at the five portals.
Attending the conduits that tunnel from the apparatus
down to the capital of her. Through the body
and its weather, to the mind and heart, to the spirit
beyond. To the mystery. And gradually to the ghosts
coming and leaving. To the difference between
the nightingale and the Japanese nightingale
which is not a nightingale. Getting lost in the treachery
of language, waylaid by the rain dancing its pavane
in the bruised light of winter afternoons.
By the flesh, luminous and transparent in the silent
clearing of her. Love as two spirits flickering
at the edge of meeting. An apartment on the third
floor without an elevator, white walls and almost
no furniture. Water seen through pine trees.
Love like the smell of basil. Richness beyond
anyone's ability to cope with. The way love is after fifty.

It was not difficult to persuade the captain
to sail a little off course and leave him
at the island. With his boxes on the sand
and the ship getting small, he was home.
Foolishly, he was disappointed that Ariel
was not amazingly there to meet him.
A part had secretly dreamed it would be a woman.
But that lasted briefly and then he was happy.
How dear the bare place looked. How good it felt
getting the supplies up to the house.

She takes off her clothes without excitement.
Her eyes don't know what to do. There is silence
in the countries of her body, Umbrian hill towns
under those small ribs, foreign voices singing
in the distance of her back. She is invisible
under the glare of her nudity. Somewhere there
is a table and the chairs she will go back to.
These men will never know what station the radio
is already set on. She will leave soon and find
herself walking in the streets with the few
people who are still awake. She will enter
her room tired and a little confused by the night.
Confused by their seeing her utterly, seeing
everything but the simple fact of her. Tomorrow
she will be in a supermarket buying potatoes
and milk, mostly naked under her dress and maybe
different. Strangers around the city will know
the delicate colors of her nipples. Some will
remember her long feet. Will she feel special
now as she sets the alarm? Is there a danger she
might feel that nothing significant happened?

TRYING

Our lives are hard to know. The gardens are provisional,
and according to which moment. Whether in the burgeoning
of July or the strict beauty of January. The language
itself is mutable. The word *way* is equally an avenue
and a matter of being. Our way into the woods
is according to the speed. To stroll into loveliness,
or leaves blowing so fast they would shred
birds in an explosion of blood. It's the Devil's
mathematics that Blake spoke of, which I failed
all three times. Everyone remembers the wonderful day
in Canada when the water was perfect. I remember
the Italian afternoon when I carried Gianna on my shoulders
in the pool, her thighs straining around my head.
My falling awkwardly and getting water in my nose.
The embarrassment forty-nine years ago which I have rejoiced in.
"To war with a god-lover is not a war," Edith Hamilton wrote,
"It is despair." What of the terribly poor Monet
scrounging for the almost empty tubes of paint his students
left. Or Watteau dying so long near Versailles. Always
the music of the court and the taste of his beautiful
goddesses constantly going away.

THE ANSWER

Is the clarity, the simplicity, an arriving
or an emptying out? If the heart persists
in waiting, does it begin to lessen?
If we are always good does God lose track
of us? When I wake at night, there is
something important there. Like the humming
of giant turbines in the high-ceilinged stations
in the slums. There is a silence in me,
absolute and inconvenient. I am haunted
by the day I walked through the Greek village
where everyone was asleep and somebody began
playing Chopin, slowly, faintly, inside
the upper floor of a plain white stone house.

The bright green of the flat fields stretching away
endlessly under the procession of great white clouds.
A ceremony without punctuation. The land empty
except for the way Chief Joseph ended just short
of the Canadian border.
                              He did not talk to them
about that, or how the tribe dwindled away amid
the immaculate silence. (As we did after
leaving college.) He did not talk to the young
about sweat lodges, or the pipe ceremony. He talked
about how America was born from the size around them,
the American mind and its spirit shaped by that
scale. They said it was just distance for them.
And boredom. How small it made them feel.

He asked about their old poetry, saying he could
not understand how it worked. They said they had never
read any of that. He talked about imagination,
as something hard. He began to hear their minds flickering.

An old woman showed him the big photographs she had
bought from the government of their great men.
She said she was one of the last three people who could
speak the language, and she would die soon. He felt
the doom everywhere. They were like a kind of whale
that was so scant it could never replace itself.
Hearing about the drunkenness and drugs and incest

each day. Then the amazing stars at night. Riding
around all day with the woman from the foundation
that had brought him there. Getting to know her
as they roamed through the ideal landscape. Lunch
and dinner together all the time. She talking about
her Irish family and growing up in New York. About
the man she lived with. Getting somebody to take
their picture. His heart flickering. His surprise.
His heart that had retired, safe in ripeness, hidden
in the light. Standing together in the terminal,
her plane straight ahead, his to the left. Both of them
stranded without a language for it.

The blue river is gray at morning
and evening. There is twilight
at dawn and dusk. I lie in the dark
wondering if this quiet in me now
is a beginning or an end.

CHERISHING WHAT ISN'T

Ah, you three women whom I have loved in this
long life, along with the few others.
And the four I may have loved, or stopped short
of loving. I wander through these woods
making songs of you. Some of regret, some
of longing, and a terrible one of death.
I carry the privacy of your bodies
and hearts in me. The shameful ardor
and the shameless intimacy, the secret kinds
of happiness and the walled-up childhoods.
I carol loudly of you among trees emptied
of winter and rejoice quietly in summer.
A score of women if you count love both large
and small, real ones that were brief
and those that lasted. Gentle love and some
almost like an animal with its prey.
What is left is what's alive in me. The failing
of your beauty and its remaining.
You are like countries in which my love
took place. Like a bell in the trees
that makes your music in each wind that moves.
A music composed of what you have forgotten.
That will end with my ending.

Not for rhyme or reason, but for the heart's
sweet seasons and her perfect back sleeping
in the morning dark.

SUDDENLY ADULT

The train's stopping wakes me.
Weeds in the gully are white
with the year's first snow.
A lighted train goes
slowly past absolutely empty.
Also going to Fukuoka.
I feel around in myself
to see if I mind. Maybe
I am lonely. It is hard
to know. It could be
hidden in familiarity.

The body is the herb,
the mind is the honey.
The heart, the heart is
the undifferentiated.
The mind touches the body
and is the sun.
The mind touches the heart
and is music.
When body touches heart
they together are the moon
in the silently falling snow
over there. Which is truth
exceeding, is the residence,
the sanctified, is the secret
closet and passes into glory.

ACKNOWLEDGMENTS

Alaska Quarterly Review
"Neglecting the Kids," "Dreaming at the Ballet"

Along These Rivers (anthology)
"A Fact," "The Danger of Wisdom"

American Poetry Review
"To Know the Invisible," "Crossing the Border, Searching for the
City," "Infectious," "Naked Without Intent," "Worth"

Columbia
"Growing up in Pittsburgh"

The Cortland Review
"Perfected"

The Dark Horse
"Living Hungry After," "The Secret," "Piecing of the Life"

The Greensboro Review
"Waking at Night"

The New Yorker
"Elegy," "The Spell Cast Over," "Summer at Blue Creek,
North Carolina," "After Love"

The Paris Review
"Painting on Plato's Wall," "Alyosha," "Winter in the Night
Fields," "Triangulating," "Ovid in Tears"

Ploughshares
"We Are the Junction"

The Quarterly
"The Difficult Beauty"

Weathered Pages (anthology)
"Everywhere and Forever," "The Answer"

*The author wishes to thank Henry Lyman
for his assistance in preparing this book.*

A NOTE ABOUT THE AUTHOR

Jack Gilbert was born in Pittsburgh. He is the author of *The Great Fires: Poems 1982–1992;*
Monolithos, which was a finalist for the Pulitzer Prize; *Views of Jeopardy,* the 1962 winner
of the Yale Younger Poets Prize; and *Refusing Heaven,* winner of the National Book Critics
Circle Award for Poetry. He also published a limited edition of elegiac poems under the title
Kochan. The recipient of a Guggenheim Fellowship and a grant from the National Endow-
ment for the Arts, Gilbert lives in Northampton, Massachusetts.

A NOTE ON THE TYPE

The text of this book was set in a typeface called Aldus, designed by the celebrated typographer Hermann Zapf in 1952–1953. Based on the classical proportion of the popular Palatino type family, Aldus was originally adapted for Linotype composition as a slightly lighter version that would read better in smaller sizes.

Hermann Zapf was born in Nuremberg, Germany, in 1918. He has created many other well-known typefaces, including Comenius, Hunt Roman, Marconi, Melior, Michelangelo, Optima, Saphir, Sistina, Zapf Book, and Zapf Chancery.

Composed by TexTech, Brattleboro, Vermont

Printed and bound by Thomson-Shore, Inc., Dexter, Michigan

Designed by Soonyoung Kwon